CREEPY CRAWLIES

LADYBUGS

by Nessa Black

AMICUS | AMICUS INK

spots

wings

Look for these
words and pictures
as you read.

claws

jaws

Have you ever seen a ladybug?

A ladybug is a big help in the garden. It eats pests. Pests can harm plants.

spots

Look at its spots.
Many ladybugs have spots.
Some do not.

wings

Look at its wings.
The soft wings help it fly.
They beat over
80 times a second!

claws

Look at its claws.
A ladybug has six claws.
They grab food.

jaws

Look at the ladybug's jaws.
They are strong.
They chew bugs.

There are 5,000
kinds of ladybugs!
They live all over the world.

spots

Look at its spots.
Many ladybugs have spots.
Some do not.

wings

Look at its wings.
The soft wings help it fly.
They beat over
80 times a second!

spots

wings

Did you find?

claws

jaws

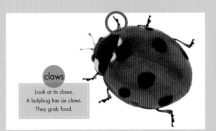

claws

Look at its claws.
A ladybug has six claws.
They grab food.

jaws

Look at the ladybug's jaws.
They are strong.
They chew bugs.

Spot is published by Amicus and Amicus Ink
P.O. Box 1329, Mankato, MN 56002
www.amicuspublishing.us

Library of Congress Cataloging-in-Publication Data
Names: Black, Nessa, author.
Title: Ladybugs / by Nessa Black.
Description: Mankato, Minnesota : Amicus, [2018] | Series:
  Spot. Creepy crawlies | Audience: K to grade 3.
Identifiers: LCCN 2016055561 (print) | LCCN 2016059927
  (ebook) | ISBN 9781681511092 (library binding) | ISBN
  9781681522289 (pbk.) | ISBN 9781681511993 (e-book)
Subjects: LCSH: Ladybugs--Juvenile literature.
Classification: LCC QL596.C65 B53 2018 (print) | LCC
  QL596.C65 (ebook) | DDC 595.76/9--dc23
LC record available at https://lccn.loc.gov/2016055561

Printed in China

HC 10 9 8 7 6 5 4 3 2 1
PB 10 9 8 7 6 5 4 3 2 1

Wendy Dieker, editor
Deb Miner, series designer
Ciara Beitlich, book designer
Holly Young, photo researcher

Photos by Dreamstime 12–13;
Getty 8–9; iStock 1, 3, 4–5, 6–7;
Shutterstock cover, 10–11, 13, 14

LADYBUGS